Duck

m**aa**tin

methuen | drama
LONDON • NEW YORK • OXFORD • NEW DELHI • SYDNEY

METHUEN DRAMA
Bloomsbury Publishing Plc
50 Bedford Square, London, WC1B 3DP, UK
1385 Broadway, New York, NY 10018, USA
29 Earlsfort Terrace, Dublin 2, Ireland

BLOOMSBURY, METHUEN DRAMA and the Methuen
Drama logo are trademarks of Bloomsbury Publishing Plc

First published in Great Britain 2024

Copyright © maatin, 2024

maatin has asserted his right under the Copyright, Designs and
Patents Act, 1988, to be identified as author of this work.

Cover design by Alice Gorman

Production photographs by Isha Shah

A catalogue record for this book is available from the British Library.

A catalog record for this book is available from the Library of Congress.

ISBN: PB: 978-1-3505-2575-7
ePDF: 978-1-3505-2576-4
eBook: 978-1-3505-2577-1

Series: Modern Plays

Typeset by Mark Heslington Ltd, Scarborough, North Yorkshire
Printed and bound in Great Britain

To find out more about our authors and books visit
www.bloomsbury.com and sign up for our newsletters.

Duck

maatin

In the name of Allah, Most Compassionate, Most Merciful.

بِسْمِ ٱللَّهِ ٱلرَّحْمَٰنِ ٱلرَّحِيمِ،

*May Allah (swt) accept my intentions, forgive my
shortcomings, and continue to guide me.*

Duck was conceived on the Hampstead Theatre's INSPIRE new writing programme. It was first performed as a virtual staged reading on 15 February 2021.

CAST

Ismail   Sid Sagar

CREATIVE

Director   Anna Himali Howard

Duck was presented as a work-in-progress as part of the Jermyn Street Theatre's Footprints Festival, performed at the Jermyn Street Theatre from 12 to 18 July 2022.

CAST

Ismail   Gavi Singh Chera

CREATIVE

Director   Imy Wyatt Corner
Sound Design   Kayode Gomez
Lighting Design   Catja Hamilton
Movement Director   Phoebe Hyder
Stage Manager   Martin Bristow

This version of *Duck* premiered at the Arcola Theatre Studio 2 on 29 June 2023, running until 15 July 2023.

CAST

Ismail   Omar Bynon

CREATIVE

Director   Imy Wyatt Corner
Producer   Katy Galloway
Set/Costume Design   Maariyah Sharjil
Sound Design/Composer   Holly Khan
Lighting Design   Jonathan Chan
Video/Projection Design   Rachel Sampley

Stage Manager	Ibraheem Hamirani
Production Manager	Chloe Stally-Gibson
Movement Director	Hamza Ali
Assistant Director	Maryam Shaharuddin
Illustrator	Aleesha Nandhra
Photography	Isha Shah
Videography	Chewboy
Social media	Elan James

An abridged version of *Duck* was performed at the Pleasance Theatre as part of the Edinburgh Festival Fringe from 31 July to 26 August 2024 and was supported by the Charlie Hartill Fund.

CAST

Ismail	Qasim Mahmood

CREATIVE

Director	Imy Wyatt Corner
Producer	Eve Allin
Set/Costume Design	Maariyah Sharjil
Sound Design/Composer	Holly Khan
Lighting Design	Jonathan Chan
Video/Projection Design	Rachel Sampley
Stage Manager	Ibraheem Hamirani
Production Managers	Chloe Stally-Gibson & Han Syles
Movement Director	Hamza Ali
Assistant Director	Maryam Shaharuddin

Following the Edinburgh Fringe, *Duck* toured in spring/summer 2025 with the support of house.

This playtext may differ slightly from the text in performance.

Special thanks

To Roy Williams, Roxana Silbert and Davina Moss, for granting me this opportunity at the beginning of my career.

To Imy Wyatt Corner, for your companionship and graft over all these years. This play belongs as much to you as it does me.

To Alba Kapoor, Mihir Bose, Duncan Stone and Miriam Walker-Khan, for lending your credibility and expertness to this idea.

To Katy Galloway, for appearing when all hope was lost, taking a leap of faith with me, and for your patience while I learnt on the job.

To Sharjil Ziauddin, for your story, and your willingness to share it.

To Alec Drysdale, Bryn Chiappe, Amy Bickersteth and Ikenna Obiekwe, for your support and counsel at all times.

To Eve Allin, for your tutelage, guidance and wisdom, and for carrying yourself with such grace at all times.

To Mohamed-Zain Dada and Suhaiymah Manzoor-Khan, for your example, your kinship, your generosity and the clarity you bring me in navigating the dunya.

To my wife, Katherine, without whom I would be capable of nothing, and who makes me feel capable of anything.

Qasim Mahmood
Ismail – Pleasance Theatre, 2024

Qasim trained at Rose Bruford.

Theatre credits include: *First Encounters: Romeo And Juliet* (RSC), *Park Life* (Birmingham Rep/Sky Comedy), *Linck & Mülhahn* (Hampstead Theatre), *Tartuffe* (Birmingham Rep), *One Man, Two Guvnors* (Liverpool Everyman/Bolton Octagon/Theatre By The Lake), *Aladdin* (Lyric Hammersmith), *Trojan Horse* (Lung Theatre).

Television credits include: *Doctors* (BBC).

Film credits include: *We Can Be Heroes* (Heroes Production).

Radio credits include: *This Little Relic* (BBC).

Omar Bynon
Ismail – Arcola Theatre, 2023

Omar is an actor, writer and workshop facilitator from East London who has an array of theatre credits including: *Blue Mist* (Royal Court), *Duck* (Arcola), *Julius Caesar* (Globe), *2036: Pawn* (Bush), *Heartfelt, Poet's Manifesto* (Stratford East).

Gavi Singh Chera
Ismail – Jermyn Street Theatre, 2022

Television credits to date of print: *Lord of the Rings: The Rings of Power* (Amazon), *The Undeclared War* (Channel 4), *The Lazarus Project* (Sky), *Vera* (ITV), and *Doctors* (BBC).

Stage credits to date: *Our Generation* (National Theatre/Chichester Festival Theatre), *Behind the Beautiful Forevers* (National Theatre), *Pygmalion* (Headlong), *The Cherry Orchard* (Yard Theatre), *1922: The Waste Land* and *Duck* (both for Jermyn Street Theatre), as well as numerous productions whilst a member of the National Youth Theatre Company, including: *Wuthering Heights*, *Consensual* and *The Merchant of Venice*.

Film credits include: *Blitz*, *Kavita and Teresa*.

Gavi has also been involved in many radio recordings for BBC Radio 4, which include, but are not limited to: *Southall Uprising*, *Comment is Free* and *Gudrun's Saga*.

maatin
Writer/Producer

maatin is an award-winning writer, dramaturg and producer who focuses on Muslim storytelling, working across theatre, radio, television and film, based between London and Los Angeles. He trained at Royal Central School of Speech and Drama (MFA in Writing for Stage and Broadcast Media, 2018–2020). His play *Friday at the masjid* is a winner of the RSC's 37 Plays, and was longlisted for The Bruntwood Prize for Playwriting 2022 and the Soho Theatre's Verity Bargate Award 2022.

Theatre credits include: *Duck* (Pleasance Theatre, 2024; Arcola Theatre, 2023; Jermyn Street Theatre, 2022) and *Metballs* (Hampstead).

Radio credits include: *Yusuf and the Whale* (BBC).

Film credits include: *Sharia's law* (Apatan Productions).

Imy Wyatt Corner
Director

Imy Wyatt Corner trained on the Drama Directing MA at Bristol Old Vic Theatre School. In 2023, she co-directed *Scotsman* Fringe First Award Winning Show *BEASTS* by Mandi Chivasa. Other directing credits include *The Last One* (Arcola Theatre), *Passing* (Park Theatre), *Scarlet Sunday* (Omnibus Theatre), *Duck* (Arcola Theatre), *A Midsummer Night's Dream* (The Grove DIY Skatepark), *Humane* (Pleasance Theatre), *Walk Swiftly & With Purpose* (North Wall Arts Centre, Theatre503), *Baby, What Blessings* (Theatre503, Bunker Theatre) and *Happy Yet?* (Edinburgh Fringe, International Theatre, Frankfurt).

Her credits as Associate/Assistant Director include *Private Lives* (West End), *Relatively Speaking* (Theatre Royal Bath, UK Tour), *The Dance of Death* (Theatre Royal Bath, UK Tour), *Love All* (Jermyn Street Theatre) and *The Straw Chair* (Finborough Theatre). She was a Creative Associate at Jermyn Street Theatre 2022/3 and is currently an Associate Artist at Arcola Theatre.

Eve Allin
Producer

Eve is a producer for theatre. She is Executive Producer at Broccoli Arts, a production company making work for/by/about lesbian, bisexual and queer people who experience misogyny. Broccoli productions include *Tender* by Eleanor Tindall and *This Might Not Be It* by Sophia Chetin-Leuner (Bush Theatre), *Salty Irina* by Eve Leigh (Paines Plough Roundabout, Summerhall), *Before I Was a Bear* by Eleanor Tindall (Soho Theatre). Eve was Associate Producer at Soho Theatre for *Super High Resolution* by Nathan Ellis in 2022 and for *Boys on the Verge of Tears* by Sam Grabiner in 2024. Independently, she is the producer for internationally award-winning artists Jaz Woodcock-Stewart (*Civilisation*), Nathan Ellis (*work.txt*) and Jennifer Jackson (*WRESTLELADSWRESTLE*). Eve is a Stage One supported producer.

Maariyah Sharjil
Set and Costume Designer

Maariyah Sharjil is a designer. She is a recent first-class graduate from BA Design for Performance at the Royal Central School of speech and Drama (2021). Before her design training, Maariyah worked at Sands Films as a costume constructor.

Her recent productions include; costume researcher for *Life of Pi* (American Repertory Theater), design associate and costume supervisor for *The P-Word* (Bush Theatre), assistant designer on *Hakawatis* (The Globe), costume designer for *The Key Workers' Cycle* (Almeida).

Jonathan Chan
Lighting Design

Jonathan trained at the Guildhall School of Music and Drama.

His credits include: *Diva: Live from Hell!* (King's Head), *Constellations* (Theatr Clwyd), *Foam* (Finborough), *Romeo & Juliet* (Polka), *Kim's Convenience* (Park), *Tiny Tim's Christmas Carol, She Stoops to Conquer* (Orange Tree), *Ignition* (Frantic Assembly), *The Flea* (Yard), *Candy* (Park), *Lady Dealer* (Paines Plough Roundabout), *An Interrogation* (Summerhall), *Love Bomb* (NYT), *Duck* (Arcola), *Grindr: the Opera* (Union), *Snowflakes* (Park & Old Red Lion), *Pussycat in Memory of Darkness* (Finborough), *In the Net* (Jermyn Street), *Grandad Me and Teddy Too* (Polka), *The Solid Life of Sugar Water* (Orange Tree), *Maybe, Probably* (Old Red Lion), *Move Fast and Break*

Things (Summerhall & Camden People's), *The Straw Chair* (Finborough), *Different Owners at Sunrise* (The Roundhouse).

Associate and assistant include: *The Passenger* R&D (Guildhall – Associate), *Fidelio* (Glyndebourne – Assistant).

Holly Khan
Sound Design/Composer

Holly is a British/Guyanese composer, sound designer and multi-instrumentalist. Creating scores for theatre, film and installation.

Most recent theatre work includes *Our Country's Good* (Lyric Hammersmith), *Sam Wu is not Afraid of Ghosts* (Polka Children's Theatre), *Sylvia* (English Theatre Frankfurt GMBH), *A Child of Science* (Bristol Old Vic), the Olivier-nominated *Blackout Songs, This Much I Know, Biscuits for Breakfast* (Hampstead Theatre), *Tess* (Turtle Key Arts/Sadler's Wells), *Dreaming and Drowning* (Bush), *I Really Do Think This Will Change Your Life* (Colchester Mercury), *Duck* (Arcola), *Northanger Abbey, Red Speedo* (Orange Tree Theatre), *The Invincibles* (Queen's Theatre Hornchurch), *Unseen Unheard* (Theatre Peckham), *Laughing Boy, Jules and Jim* (Jermyn Street Theatre), *Mansfield Park* (The Watermill), *The Beach House* (Park Theatre), *For A Palestinian* (Bristol Old Vic/Camden People's Theatre) *OFFIE nominated for Best Sound Design*, *Amal Meets Alice* (Good Chance Theatre Company, The Story Museum), *Kaleidoscope* (Filskit Theatre Company, Southbank Centre/Oxford Playhouse).

Ibraheem Hamirani
Stage Manager

Ibraheem grew up in Oman and is a London-based stage manager. He is a graduate in Stage Management from the Royal Birmingham Conservatoire. His credits include *La Bohème* (OperaUpClose), *Scoring A Century* (British Youth Opera), *The Tempest* (Wildcard's productions), *An Inspector Calls* (PW Productions), *Bad Roads* (Fourth Monkey Productions), *Duck* (Two Magpies Productions), *Rumble In The Jungle* (Rematch), *Scarlet Sunday* (Aslant Theatre Company) and *Fabulous Creatures* (Collide Theatre Company). He is extremely excited and grateful to be a part of this production.

Hamza Ali
Movement Director

Hamza is an inter-disciplinary movement artist. With a background in professional sports coaching and devised theatre-making, he combines physical performance with creative expression to create, direct and perform movement. In 2024, he was resident director for Dante or Die's *Kiss Marry Kill*. Previous movement credits include *10 Nights* (UK tour), *Going For Gold* (Chelsea Theatre), *For One More Day to Live* (Theatre Peckham), *Daytime Deewane* (Half Moon Theatre) and *Statues* (Barbican). He has staged two successful original productions, *Bhai* (The Place) and *1518* (Edinburgh Fringe Festival). A recipient of the Embassy Scholarship, he graduated with an MA in Movement from the Royal Central School of Speech and Drama in 2021 and continues to movement direct for the BA Acting MT course as a visiting professional.

Maryam Shaharuddin
Assistant Director

A youth and community facilitator, Maryam co-creates theatre with participants in the UK and Malaysia. She has delivered workshops and performances at a range of organisations including Angel Shed, Kiln, Almeida, Bush, PositivelyUK, Company Three and the National Theatre. She is also an Associate Artist at Coney, focusing on a practice of playful activism with communities. Her assistant directing credits include *Daytime Deewane* (Half Moon) and *Duck* (Arcola). She has worked as an engagement producer for *This Might Not Be It* and *Statues* (Bush Theatre). She is also currently a mentor for Tamasha's Creative Wellbeing Lab, sharing her practice in arts and health. Joy and play are at the heart of her practice in creating inclusive, socially engaged theatre. Maryam is especially passionate about making work that celebrates and elevates the stories of Muslim Women.

Supported using public funding by the National Lottery through Arts Council England.

Supported using public funding by
ARTS COUNCIL ENGLAND

www.pleasance.co.uk

PLEASANCE THEATRE TRUST

The Pleasance has been at the heart of Fringe theatre and comedy since 1985. With an international profile and a network of alumni that reads like a who's who of contemporary comedy, drama and entertainment, the Pleasance is a place for the experimental and the new.

The Pleasance is both a Festival Organisation of 27 temporary venues across three sites, and a London theatre and development centre, with two permanent performance spaces which operate year-round. The Pleasance in London and Edinburgh are entirely symbiotic. We've been a registered charity since 1995 in England and Wales and 2012 in Scotland, supporting opportunities for artists year round.

THE CHARLIE HARTILL FUND

The Charlie Hartill Fund supports UK-based theatre makers and comedians in bringing their work to the Edinburgh Festival Fringe.

Our flagship fund offers unique and unparalleled support to artists through direct cash investment, programming and mentoring support. Through the fund, we hope to remove the financial risk for companies and allow creativity to take centre stage.

The fund was established in 2004 in memory of Charlie Hartill.

TWO MAGPIES
PRODUCTIONS

Two Magpies Productions is a new production company from maatin, an award-winning writer focused on telling Muslim stories.

First and foremost, we believe in the urgent need for a radical transformation of both the creative arts industry and the world, towards a more just and more equal future for all.

Further, that we live in a society that is structurally anti-Muslim, which therefore must be given consideration to in all areas of our work.

This is at the heart of everything we do.

We prioritise those from marginalised and minoritised identities, to create opportunities for those who remain underrepresented in the creative arts.

In particular, we desire to centre Muslimness, for all its breadth, range and meaning to those who identify with it, and look to increase the participation of Muslims in all areas of the creative process.

We will only make work in a safe environment that protects workers, upholding the highest standards of professionalism, labour rights, dignity and access.

Foreword

I was very lucky to write this play in one of the most beautiful places I've ever spent time in – Sun Valley, Idaho – upon the unceded territory of the Shoshone, Bannock and Lemhi tribes. It's about as far removed from the world of the play as you could imagine, and yet provided the perfect backdrop for inspiration. It's true what they say about the natural world and creativity. More than four years on, entirely by chance, I happen to be writing these notes in the very same place. I hope it continues to be a place of creative significance for me for years to come.

* * *

I was invited to join the Hampstead Theatre Writers' Group on 28 February 2020. In the innumerable applications, competitions and programmes I have submitted to, both before and since, I don't think I have ever been more nervous or hopeful for the outcome. Honestly, I pinned my entire career and worth on it, which was an incredibly naïve thing to do, especially since I was still in drama school at the time! Looking back, not only have I learned that there is a healthy amount of luck and good fortune involved in these things, but that each moment of success or failure ends up being extremely fleeting when set against the overall of one's career.

As we now know, days later, the entire world completely shifted. I had a serious case of COVID-19, bringing life into sharp focus. By the time I eventually sat down to write the first draft of *Duck*, I had recovered, written an entirely different play (my first), finished drama school and got married.

Duck, conceived when theatres were dark, in the midst of uncertainty with no determinable future ahead, has gone on to become the engine of my career to date. This one play has already given me more than I ever imagined or hoped for. Now, I hope that the text can be another way to further my overarching goal, to create more opportunities for Muslims and other minoritised backgrounds in every area of this industry.

* * *

What does it mean to be a Muslim writer? It's a term I use to describe myself, without feeling remotely comfortable with it. I can only offer insights into the considerations, questions and thoughts that I have faced. They don't necessarily follow a logical or conclusive pathway.

Nor are they necessarily the same thoughts that another Muslim writer would have – I am just one Muslim, one writer.

Contradictions feel dangerous as a Muslim in the West. When you spend your life with such close scrutiny on your identity, it leaves little room. And yet here I was. Having thought I had complete clarity in my commitment to write stories featuring Muslim characters in ways that moved beyond damaging, inaccurate, confined stereotypes, at the first time of asking, I had pitched a play set against the backdrop of the events of 7/7.

Not only was this a massive contradiction, but it felt like a complete betrayal of myself and everything I was working towards. And beyond that, bearing a weight that every Muslim, exposed to entrenched, state-backed and targeted ignorance, anger, surveillance and criminalisation, was vulnerable to my choices. A delusional idea but one that was too consequential to ignore.

I've sat with this feeling throughout the stages of development of this play. To be a Muslim writer is to have to ask yourself these things, over and over, without many places to look for the answers. I've changed my mind many times. My greatest fear has been the risk of failure, that my choices are the wrong ones. It's hard not to worry that I'll be judged for them, or that I'll only get one chance at this, and I've blown it.

Creativity from a place of fear does not bode well. In the intervening years, I have found a growing number of peers with whom to share this work and these questions. From those conversations have come reassurances and validations that are incredibly helpful, practical and comforting. I am so proud now that *Duck*, as expressed by a fellow playwright, exists in conversation with other plays that address similar themes and subjects. It's something I was striving for without realising I could ever have it.

* * *

Ultimately, I had the truth to fall back on. The play is loosely based on my own experiences as a teenager attending a public school, and my encounters with a teacher that took a particular dislike to me for no discernible reason. More importantly, those experiences, and the story of Ismail in *Duck*, are sadly very commonplace. To me, the power of this play is not necessarily in the specific story, but its ubiquity. Being able to reflect the feeling that one can recall from their own lives is the truth I sought to capture. My hope is that resonance creates an opportunity to heal.

Finally, the choice to set *Duck* in this specific time and place provided the grounding I desired to scrutinise the urgent nature of Islamophobia in our present society. 7/7 can be considered the beginning, or one of the most significant events, in the past two decades that has seen state-led anti-Muslimness run rampant and be entirely normalised within Britain. As one such example, in 2016, Conservative candidate for Mayor Zac Goldsmith used imagery from 7/7 to try to persuade Londoners against voting for his Muslim opponent, Sadiq Khan.

By setting the play in and around this pivotal summer, we get to exist in two times simultaneously. In 2005, living through Ismail's eyes, watching how the events both affect him in the moment, and foreshadowing their impact on his future. And we literally and physically exist in the present, with the spectre of knowledge and the reality of what it means to be Muslim in Britain today.

* * *

When first writing this play, the pandemic laid bare the injustices of our society in an unignorable way. Optimistically, I hoped this would spark urgently needed systemic change. Instead, corruption, white supremacy, colonialism and elitism further embedded themselves. Lessons were not learnt.

Now, a genocide of the Palestinian people is taking place with support and funding from all major Western powers. For those of us who stand with Palestine, we exist in permanent heartbreak for our brothers and sisters who deserve life and freedom. Voicing our desire for the liberation of Palestine can feel like a risk, particularly for Muslims, but it is the absolute minimum we can and must do. I write this here in the hope that anyone who reads these words and who shares these feelings finds strength and solidarity in them. May they remind us to take sustained and further action, until these words become redundant, and Palestine is free.

For my father, Faarid Hashim Patel, for sharing his love of cricket with me, and for responding to the challenges of this world with a pure heart and humble intentions.

Duck

'What do they know of cricket who only cricket know?'

– C.L.R. James

Characters

Ismail – *14/15, British Indian, Muslim, male*

Setting

London. 2005.

Notes

The entire play is narrated by Ismail. All other characters are his interpretations of them. There are two fictional commentators who exist solely in Ismail's head. They're named after the famous duo of Mark Nicholls and Richie Benaud, and like in a traditional sports commentary booth, they converse with one another. These lines are intended to be pre-recorded.

Lines in ' ' are direct speech by Ismail to other characters. Other characters only speak directly to one another and are therefore not indicated with ' '.

Lines without ' ' are narration.

// indicates a new location or shift in time.

Scene One

7 July 2005. The duck pond at St. James's Park. Morning. It's quiet on a warm, sunny, summer day.

Ismail*, wearing school uniform, relaxes on the grass. He tears off pieces of bread from a loaf and forms balls. He lobs them aimlessly towards the ducks.*

Ismail   First lesson on Thursday morning is double Latin. Sir never takes the register. I don't even mind Latin . . .

He shrugs and looks at the blue sky.

Ismail   Almost the end of the year anyway. Barely any work going on. Everyone's probably begged to have our lesson in the quad.

He feels judged.

Ismail   Look, who'd feed you if I wasn't here? Exactly.

There's no response from the ducks.

Ismail   I need time to think. Without everyone trying to tell me what to do, or give me detention, or tell me I'm wrong.

You don't say anything.

I can breathe. It's helping. I think.

Ismail *brushes off the feeling. He stands up, and takes a few deliberate paces, mimicking the behaviour of a cricket fast bowler.*

Commentator *(V/O)*   Well, Richie, it looks like Smiley Akhtar's coming on to bowl now. Known better of course for his unmatched wizardry with the bat, but he's taken a few wickets here and there.

I believe there was a hattrick in his first ever school match, Mark!

My, that's some start to a career, isn't it? Is there anything the boy can't do?

Ismail *runs in to bowl, releasing his bread ball into the air.*

Commentator (*V/O*)   It's a well-pitched ball, and – yep, that's a duck!

Ismail *jumps up, hands outstretched.*

Ismail   HOWZAAAAT!

Ismail *waits in desperate expectation, appealing to an imaginary umpire.*

Commentator (*V/O*)   Ha ha ha! Very good, Richie! A duck!

There was so much promise in Smiley Akhtar's career, Mark. The best timing of any school cricketer I've ever seen, at such a young age. What happened?

Ismail   Let *me* explain it!

Ismail *sits back down and returns to tossing bread aimlessly.*

Ismail   I just need to think.

It's not entirely clear to whom that's directed.

Ismail   Best I go back to the beginning of term.

Ismail *gets up. He takes off his school tie and blazer, and kicks off his shoes.*

Scene Two

May 2005. A leafy, upper-middle-class home in St. John's Wood, Northwest London. **Ismail***'s bedroom.*

It's the night before the beginning of term. **Ismail** *packs his cricket bag.*

Ismail   I'm never this happy about holidays being over. But summer term starting means cricket season is finally here. I can't wait!

He picks up his beloved cricket bat.

Ismail   This bat's seen it all.

He examines the cherries adorning the bat.

Ismail   Isle of Wight tour, Year Eight.

Commentator (*V/O*)   Smiley's creamed a cover drive that's racing towards the boundary. They're going to win the match! Smiley raises his bat. Here come his teammates. They're carrying him off the pitch!

He points at another.

Ismail   I'm pretty sure this one, I hit a six so big, it smashed a car window. Oops!

He wields the bat like it's an extension of him.

Ismail   Last year, I had the most runs in a season, highest average, most innings not out, most fifties. And my maiden century!

He raises his bat in salute to an imaginary crowd.

Ismail   This season was going to be even better. No Year Ten has ever played for the school's First XI before. In more than two hundred years! Until me.

He considers the weight of it all.

Ismail   The Firsts got to wear special blazers on match days with the school's crest. Use the big pitch with massive boundaries and a proper scoreboard. Skip school for all-day matches and away games around the whole country. And the pavilion! Exclusively for the Firsts, with its own room for tea. It was like being a proper cricketer. A professional.

My dad walks in.

Dad   There's my little master!

Dad *ruffles* **Ismail***'s hair. He pulls away.*

Ismail   'The Little Master' is the nickname of Indian cricket legend, Sachin Tendulkar. Small in size, humungous in talent and reputation, worshipped by all Indians, my dad no exception. He talks about Sachin Tendulkar so much, I think he secretly wishes I'd go up in a puff of smoke and come back as him. You know, like on *Stars in Their Eyes*.

Spotlight on **Ismail**.

Ismail   'Tonight, Matthew, I'm going to be . . . SACHIN TENDULKAR!'

Canned cheering and applause. Blackout. Exit **Ismail**.

Smoke fills the stage. Lights flash. Loud, thumping music. Big sliding doors open.

Enter **Ismail**, *dressed as Sachin Tendulkar. He starts playing shots, holding the finish, posing. He salutes the crowd with his bat, removes his helmet, regards, then kisses the Indian logo on it before holding his helmet and bat aloft above his head. He soaks in the glory.*

The smoke clears, the lights and applause stop abruptly. **Ismail** *is snapped back to reality.*

Ismail   'I wish you'd stop calling me that.'

Dad   Pssht. You should feel flattered to be compared to Sachin, Ismail. What an artist! His footwork, his timing . . .

Ismail   Once he starts on Tendulkar, there's no stopping him.

Dad   . . . There isn't a bowler in the world who can outsmart the little master!

Ismail   'I'm almost fifteen. I'm not little.'

Dad   It's a nickname. My father called me *ladoo* all my life. When you were a baby, we used to call you *gulab jamun*.

Ismail   'Why can't you just call me Smiley like everyone else?'

Dad   Smiley?! What are you, a clown?! You should be proud of your name.

Ismail *rolls his eyes.*

Ismail   'No one can pronounce it!'

Dad   All your friends with all that education and they can't pronounce a name like Ismail? Their parents should ask for a refund.

Ismail   He laughs at his own joke, then hands me something. It's a card with a verse from the Quran.

Dad   For your bag.

Ismail   'I don't need any luck, Dad.'

Dad   It's not for luck, Ismail! Don't forget where all this came from. Remember, Allah can take it away whenever He likes.

Ismail *takes the card and slips it into his bag.*

Ismail   'As long as it helps me get into *Wisden*!'

Dad   *Insha'Allah.*

Ismail   *Wisden*. The yellow book of cricketing immortality. Every year, its hundreds of wafer-thin pages and tiny font provided an account of everything and anything that happened in cricket that year, even school matches. With a few big scores, I could get my name in there . . .

Ismail *becomes lost in his fantasy.*

Ismail (*as he imagines the author of* Wisden)   The name Smiley Akhtar might give the impression that this young chap is amiable and friendly. But he's no friend to bowlers, fast or spin alike. In fact, the lightning reactions of this wunderkind talent imply an almost superhuman ability to pick up line and length almost before the ball has left the bowler's hand. Every shot in the arsenal, played with textbook preciseness and measured aggression, Akhtar is likely to have opponents tossing in their nightmares in anticipation of facing him next season, after taking apart school after school. It's enough to put a smile on any spectator's face . . .

Dad Ismail! Ismail!

Ismail*'s brought back down to Earth.*

Dad We're so proud of you, *badshah*. But you mustn't let cricket affect your schoolwork. Your education comes first.

Ismail 'I know, I know.'

Dad Don't waste the opportunity you've been given.

Ismail This was a recurring speech. How lucky I was to go to such a prestigious school. What doors it would open up for me.

Dad Who knows, you could be the first Indian Prime Minster of this country one day.

Ismail My whole life being mapped out for me. I'm fourteen!

My dad smiles and gives me a big hug. I know they only want the best for me, it's just sometimes, it feels like a lot of pressure to live up to. It's not like that with cricket. Where anything seems possible.

Dad Don't forget to say your *kalima* before bed.

Ismail He leaves.

Ismail *paces around the room, tossing a ball to himself.*

Ismail Tomorrow can't come any quicker. But I'm too excited to fall asleep. I see the light's still on in my dadi's – my grandma's – room.

He peeks in.

Ismail She's sitting quietly on her bed. She sees me lingering and smiles, calling me inside.

He sits down next to her. They hold hands.

Ismail She doesn't speak English. And I can't speak any Urdu. When we hang out, mostly I just tell her about my cricket matches. I don't think she seems to mind. I describe every single shot, run and incident, and she listens.

We sit for a while. I watch her watch the news on TV with the sound off. Every so often she squeezes my hand tightly. She's remarkably strong for such a tiny old woman.

Out of her window, just across the road, I can see the grandstands of Lord's. The Home of Cricket. In a couple of months, England would be playing in the Ashes, right there. What a summer it was going to be.

Scene Three

The next day. School. Lunchtime is approaching.

Ismail *is desperate for the lesson to end. The teacher drones on.*

Ismail   It's like Sir is deliberately dragging this out for as long he humanly can.

Ismail *hangs off his seat.*

Ismail   I could swear this clock has stopped.

'Sir, I think it's lunchtime?'

Sir   Thank you, Smiley. I'm very capable of telling the time.

Ismail   Ugh. I look over at my best friend, Finn. He's in a trance, staring out the window. Blue skies on the first day of the season?! *Allahu akbar!*

Ismail *whispers to* **Finn**.

Ismail   'Can he just hurry up already?'

Finn   Classic.

Ismail   Finn's the second-best player in our year. We've had some epic partnerships over the years.

Finn   You excited?

Ismail *puffs out his chest and grins.*

Ismail   'Can't bloody wait.'

Sir   Ssshhh!

They quieten down for barely a moment.

Finn   I'm so jealous.

Ismail   'Guess where we get to go for the cricket tour.'

Finn   Go on . . .

Ismail   'BARBADOS!'

All winter long, all those cold and wet nights lugging my cricket bag on the tube back and forth for nets, I'd been dreaming of Barbados. Two weeks of sun, sand and morning-till-night cricket.

Finn   Oh my god. You're so lucky!

Ismail   'It's going to be incredible.'

Finn   By the way, Dad's got a whole load of tickets to the Ashes. You wanna go?

Ismail   'Duh! Thanks, mate.'

Sir   Would you keep it down back there?!

They lower their voices but keep going.

Finn   You know, I reckon we can do it.

Ismail   'England haven't won the Ashes since before we were born!'

Finn   I'm telling you, this year is our year.

Ismail   'If you say so.'

Big Ben strikes one.

Ismail   Finally!

He races out of the classroom.

//

Outside the pavilion. **Ismail** *looks up at the historic building.*

Ismail   I've spent the last two years wondering what it would be like. To walk out, pads on, through the little white gate, to the middle. Just like a professional.

He takes a deep breath and enters. It's sparse, wooden, musty, full of charm, steeped in tradition. He surveys the room.

Ismail   The walls are lined with the names of every team going back a hundred years at least?! Some are so faded I can barely make them out. Mine's going to be alongside them. Wow.

Ismail *pads up.*

Ismail   There's literally nothing I don't love about playing cricket. Ever since I can remember, I've been obsessed.

Commentator *(V/O)*   Thanks, folks, for tuning into another evening's coverage of Hallway Cricket. We're picking up the action with Smiley Akhtar coming into bat. I believe he's . . . yes that's right, still the record holder for most runs scored before bedtime.

Young **Ismail** *plays a controlled shot along the ground.*

Commentator *(V/O)*   Wonderful straight bat there from Smiley, Mark. I believe his dad is responsible for that impeccable technique.

Ismail   When I was a bit older, my dadi became my personal cricket coach. Any time the sun was out, we'd be in the garden. We had this perfect strip of flat grass, a homemade wicket. She'd toss a tennis ball to me, underarm. It was too easy.

Young **Ismail** *spanks it all over the garden, running back and forth between the wickets.*

Commentator *(V/O)*   Smiley's creamed another one to the far corner towards the rhododendrons! Off goes grandma into the bushes. She's going to have a hard time finding it. Smiley's racking up the runs here, Richie! I've lost count!

Ismail   I'd score at least a hundred by sunset every day.

Young **Ismail** *hits one over the house. He admires it.*

Commentator (*V/O*)   And this one's gone clean over the house! I think it's in the road!

Ismail   I'd been made captain of the school team, every year. My mum and dad were so proud. They couldn't make it to many games, but the day I scored my first fifty, there they were, sat on the boundary, cheering me on.

Commentator (*V/O*)   What a moment. That shot brings up a half-century in just twenty-two balls. He's carried his bat from the top of the innings. Life is good for Smiley Akhtar, isn't it, Mark?

Ismail *grabs his helmet and bat and exits the pavilion with a spring in his step. He looks out at the pitch, breathing in the fresh-cut grass smell.*

Ismail   What a day for it.

Across the other side, I can see the rest of the team gathering besides the nets, fresh whites sparkling in the sunshine. They're in a semi-circle, hands cupped, knees bent. Someone stands in the middle, wielding an old, weathered bat, sending catches flying in every direction.

When you watch cricket from a distance, there's a trick of the eye. A split-second delay that comes after ball hits bat before you hear the sound of leather against willow. The margin between the speed of light and the speed of sound. It's a beautiful thing.

Time to get started.

He jogs over to the nets.

Ismail   As I get near, the captain of the Firsts, Pimmers, calls out.

Pimmers   It's the new kid!

Ismail *raises his bat and curtseys. The others cheer.*

Pimmers Bit keen, are you, Smiley?

Ismail I can hear a few laughs. I'm the only one in my pads. Tossers. I can take their shit because I'm better than almost all of them, I reckon.

Commentator *(V/O)* Smiley's about half the size of the others, wouldn't you say, Mark? Wonder how he'll keep up with the older chaps.

Just like the great Sachin Tendulkar has been showing his whole career, stature has two meanings, eh?

Ismail *grins.*

Ismail 'Yeah. I'm here to teach you all how to bat.'

Pimmers Come on then!

Ismail *makes his way down to the bottom of the nets.*

Ismail Nets might be the place I'm happiest in the world. All alone with my thoughts and no one to bother me. All the joking and chatting's going on at the bowler's end, but down here, it's peace and calm.

He presses his feet into the spongey astroturf and straightens the rickety metal stumps. Like he's done a thousand times before.

Ismail They say cricket's a team game. But come on. You're out there, all alone. Batsman v bowler. Just how I like it.

He bounces up and down, then takes his stance.

Ismail 'Let's have it!'

A ball comes in. **Ismail** *plays a perfect cover drive.*

Ismail A few of them gather, trying to bowl as aggressively as possible at me. No matter.

Ismail *dispatches shot after shot.*

Ismail   'Is that the best you've got?!'

He looks across the pitch.

Ismail   I've just cracked one straight back over the bowler's head, when out of the corner of my eye, I see a teacher running across the pitch towards us, waving his arms like a mad man. He's screaming at the top of his lungs. He comes flying in, loses his footing and crashes into the nets.

Ismail *laughs.*

Eagles   EXCUSE ME!! EXCUSE ME!! WHAT DO YOU THINK YOU'RE DOING?!

Eagles *catches his breath.*

Eagles   What do you think you're doing, boy? Get out of there. HURRY UP!

Ismail *shuffles up to the top of the nets.*

Ismail   I've got no idea who this man even is.

Eagles   Who told you to start batting? What are the rules about batting in the nets?

Ismail   'I don't know /'

Eagles   You don't know? You cannot bat in these nets without a teacher or coach present.

Ismail   Yes you can. OK maybe technically you're not meant to, but no one gives a toss about that! And it wasn't like I wasn't wearing my helmet. This was uncalled for.

Eagles   What's your name, boy?

Ismail   He fixes his eyes on me. They're dark and narrow.

'Smiley, Sir.'

Eagles   Smiley? What sort of name is that?

Ismail   My face feels really hot.

'It's Ismail, Sir. Everyone just calls me Smiley.'

Eagles   Well, Smiley, go and take your pads off. You're done for the day.

Commentator (*V/O*)   Oh dear, Mark! Looks like Smiley's been sent for an early bath. Seems like a harsh punishment.

Ismail   'I'm sorry, Sir, but why? I haven't done anything.'

Eagles   Because I'm in charge and I say so.

Commentator (*V/O*)   He isn't messing around, Richie. He's wagging his finger rather close to Smiley's face, don't you think?

I agree, bit of an overreaction from the teacher there.

Ismail   Who is he? And why am I the only one getting in trouble for this?

He looks around at the others.

Ismail   No one speaks up. Some are hiding their smiles, others are looking away.

Silence. **Ismail** *shrugs and walks off. He sheds his pads.*

Ismail   I watch from a distance as the rest of the team gathers around.

Eagles   Well then! Start of a new season! Great day for it! I'm delighted to be the new First XI coach.

Ismail   What the hell? He's our coach? Where's Mr Campbell?

Eagles   My name is Mr Eagles. As some of you might know, this is a team I'm quite familiar with. Here's a hint. You may have spotted my name up in the pavilion.

Ismail   He went here?

Eagles   It was my greatest honour to represent our school as a member of this team. That's something I hope you'll take as seriously as me.

Ismail   I slope back over to join them. Pimmers smirks at me.

Pimmers   Hard luck, Smiley. He's a bit of a tough one, isn't he?

Ismail   'Why didn't anyone say anything? You lot were all bowling at me.'

Pimmers *laughs*.

Pimmers   Don't be a snitch, Smiley. You're with the big boys now. Bit of advice. Eagles holds the school batting record. He's a legend. Best to stay on his good side.

Ismail   I knew it! I'd looked up the school records, setting my sights on smashing them. Most runs scored in a season, 1,425, held by J.T. Eagles.

'What happened to Mr Campbell?'

Pimmers   No clue.

Ismail   Mr Campbell had invited me down to winter training. Who put me in the team. And now he's gone.

Before I have a chance to process any of this, Eagles appears.

Eagles   You're not upset about before, are you? I'm here to make sure everyone keeps their heads on, that's all. No hard feelings, eh, boy?

Ismail   He ruffles my hair.

Ismail *steps back, alarmed*.

Eagles   Come on, boy, I thought they called you Smiley?

Ismail   Why does he keep calling me boy? This time he goes for my shoulder, giving it a squeeze. It's quite painful actually.

Commentator *(V/O)*   Strange situation developing here, Richie. Smiley Akhtar, fresh off his promotion to the school's

top team, seems to have fallen out with new coach Mr
Eagles.

Very strange indeed, Mark. What'll this do for Smiley's place
in the team, you have to wonder.

Ismail *takes a deep breath.*

Ismail   I need to be on his good side.

He forces a big smile.

Ismail   'Yes, Sir. Sorry about before. Misunderstanding.'

Eagles   No harm done, boy. These rules are for your safety,
remember that.

Ismail   Yeah, yeah. Whatever. Enough with the lesson
already.

Another big, fake smile.

Ismail   'Absolutely, Sir. Understood. I'm really excited
about joining the team. In fact, I'd love to chat about my
place in the batting order.'

His eyes narrow on me again. It's funny, he sort of looks like
an actual eagle.

Eagles   I'll be putting up a team sheet on Friday based on
today's nets.

Ismail   'Yes Sir. It's just, you won't have seen me bat
today . . .'

Eagles   Yes, well, we both know whose fault that is, don't
we?

Ismail   He's smirking as he says it! He squeezes my
shoulder again. Ow! I can feel tears forming.

Eagles   You look so serious, boy! This is cricket! Live up to
your name and smile a bit.

Ismail   At this point, I'm convinced this man has been sent
here to ruin my life.

Ismail *makes a weak attempt at another smile.*

Eagles   Good. Now get in there and let's have a look at your bowling.

He sizes **Ismail** *up, a bit creepily.*

Eagles   I bet you bowl a spicy googly, don't you?

Commentator *(V/O)*   Looks like Mr Eagles might be a bit confused, Mark. Smiley's not much of a spin bowler. Not sure what's given him that impression.

Scene Four

A few days later. Home.

It's **Ismail**'s *fifteenth birthday. He holds a bright yellow cake.*

Ismail   Fifteen today. The big one-five. Every year, my mum goes all out. She's baked me my own copy of *Wisden*!

He shows off the cake. It looks like a copy of Wisden Cricketers' Almanack.

Ismail   My dad's been collecting actual *Wisdens* for years. They line an entire shelf in his study. He has this incredible ability to memorise crazy facts and figures from them. Imagine next year, when he'll be able to look up my name in the 2005 edition.

Dad   Ismail, did you know, when Sachin was in school, he and Vinod Kambli put on SIX HUNDRED AND SIXTY FOUR RUNS!

Ismail   OK, so mostly he just remembers facts about Sachin.

'I know, Dad. You've told me before.'

Dad   And Sachin made THREE HUNDRED AND TWENTY-SIX, NOT OUT!

Ismail   'Yes, Dad.'

He smiles and hands me a long, thin, package.

Dad   Happy birthday, *beta*.

Ismail *weighs it up.*

Ismail   Here. We. Go! The Newbery Hammer was the lightest, most powerful bat ever made. I'd been dropping hints about it for months. Half the England team had one!

He unwraps it carefully.

Ismail   With this bat, I was going to score 1,426 runs, beat Mr Eagles' school record, and get into *Wisden*.

He continues unwrapping, eventually unsheathing a brand new cricket bat. He holds it up, eyes wide. He runs his hand along its smooth blade. He smells it. He turns it over and looks at the name emblazoned on it. He stops, puzzled.

Ismail   'MRF?'

He's crestfallen.

Ismail   Wait a minute. This was not what I had asked for.

He turns to his dad.

Ismail   'Dad, what's this?'

Dad   It's the exact same bat that Sachin uses!

Ismail   It's a sickness, I'm telling you.

'But what about the Newbery?'

Dad   Newbery, shmoo-bery! This is proper craftsmanship, *beta*. I had this sent from India just for my little master.

Ismail   'I'm not little! I'm fifteen.'

Dad   Quite right. My *badshah* is all grown up.

Ismail *looks at the bat again.*

Ismail   I'd already gone around boasting that I was getting a Newbery. What were the others going to say when I showed up with . . . this?

My dad, meanwhile, is grinning from ear to ear. I can't tell him. It'll break his heart.

Ismail *offers up a paltry smile.*

Ismail   Thanks.

He puts the bat aside.

//

Later. They watch TV.

Ismail   Finn comes round and joins us for our annual viewing of *Lagaan*. It's my favourite. In it, a group of Indian villagers challenge their British rulers to a cricket match. At the end, the hero hits a six with the last ball to win the match. Oops, spoiler. Dadi's glued to the action. I think Hindi films remind her of home.

Dad   Psst. Show Finn your new bat, Ismail.

Ismail   Ugh. He's so embarrassing.

'Not now, Dad.'

Finn   Oh, go on Smiley! Did you get the Newbery?

Ismail   My dad can't wait a second longer to show off the MRF.

Dad   Even better! I got Ismail the same bat that Tendulkar uses.

Finn *checks it out.*

Finn   Love it!

He gives it a few air swings. **Ismail** *grabs it back.*

Ismail   Hey! Careful. I haven't knocked it in yet.

Awkward.

Finn   So, you excited for the Ashes, Mr Akhtar?

Dad   England don't stand a chance against Ponting! Brett Lee bowls a hundred miles an hour! He's the Kangaroo Express!

Finn   Oh, come on! We've got a really good chance I think.

Dad   I don't know. Michael Vaughan's not my cup of tea.

Ismail   I can feel my face getting hot. I don't want my dad to offend Finn.

'Dad, Finn's taking me to the final Test.'

Dad   How lovely!

Finn   You not much of an England fan then, Mr Akhtar?

Dad   I'm an admirer of cricketing greatness, no matter the jersey. But yes, in this house, our hearts beat for India.

Finn   Smiley, I thought you supported England?

Ismail   Just as I feel like I'm about to explode with embarrassment, my dadi shoves a giant Tupperware full of leftovers into Finn's lap.

Ismail *leaps up.*

Ismail   'Can everyone just stop being SO ANNOYING!'

There's a long, pregnant silence. He sits back down.

Ismail   'We're going to miss the best part.'

He smiles in his grandma's direction.

Commentator *(V/O)*   I'm not sure he's convinced anyone with that excuse!

They continue watching in silence.

Ismail   Every time Finn's dad takes us to a match, he asks me who I support. I always think it's weird that he keeps forgetting. But even when I say England, he gives me this look, as if it's a joke. I don't get it.

Scene Five

A week later. Cricket pavilion.

It's the first match of the season. **Ismail**, *pads on, searches his cricket bag in a hurry.*

Ismail   Uh oh. This is not good.

He keeps rummaging.

Commentator *(V/O)*   Let's have another look at that wicket, Richie. It looks like Greggers completely switched off there. Poor timing and an easy catch for the man at slip. One hundred and twenty-two for six now, still fifty-four short of their target. Is Smiley Akhtar, the next man in at number eight, going to be able to steer them to an unlikely win here? So far, there's no sign of the debutant.

Ismail   'I'm coming!'

Commentator *(V/O)*   Smiley is, of course, making history today. Just celebrated his fifteenth birthday! My, they just get younger and younger, don't they?

Ismail *keeps looking. He's sweating.*

Ismail   I could always just not wear one. (*Thinking.*) Andrew did that once. Ended up in A&E with what looked like a third ball. Blood and everything.

A protective box flies across the stage. **Ismail** *sticks up his hand and catches it. He looks at it and hesitates. He winces and shoves it inside his underwear. The cold plastic has him hopping around.*

Ismail   This is not how I imagined this moment.

He runs out to the crease, panting. He tries to settle down. He fiddles with his crotch.

Ismail   It's too big. What's wrong with this thing? It's sloshing around and digging into me at the same time.

He looks up at the bowler.

Ismail   The bowler's massive!

He turns to the wicketkeeper.

Ismail   'How old's this guy, then?'

Wicketkeeper   He's got a trial for England.

Ismail *looks a bit nervy. He signals to the umpire, taking guard.*

Commentator (*V/O*)   Smiley surveying the field here. It's never a nice thing facing down your first ball, is it, Richie? I know I always hated it.

Ismail   I've been sat around all innings. Batting eight! I've never come in lower than four in my life.

He prepares for the ball.

Ismail   Never mind. This is my chance. Time to save the day.

Commentator (*V/O*)   The bowler's coming in. Smiley will be looking to get off the mark quickly here.

The ball comes in. It's quick. **Ismail** *is surprised by the pace and shuffles backwards. The ball whistles by.*

Ismail   Whoa!

Commentator (*V/O*)   Was that a leave, Richie? Looks like he might have misjudged that one. Bit more pace than he's used to, perhaps?

Ismail *fiddles around.*

Ismail   I watch the ball make its way back around. Mr Trial For England's got a twenty-step run up! Eagles is umpiring. He's fiddling with the counting stones in his white jacket. Smirking, as usual. Dick.

He practises the shot he wants to play.

Ismail   Get on the front foot. Trust my timing. Don't be scared.

He steps back in. The bowler runs in again.

Commentator *(V/O)*   Here comes the next ball. Let's see what Smiley can do.

Ismail   I'm gripping my bat so tightly.

He flinches and shuffles backwards. Too late. The ball clatters into the stumps.

Commentator *(V/O)*   And he's clean bowled him, Richie! Totally beaten for pace.

Ismail   I hear the clip of ball on wicket and the thud as the bails hit the ground. The wicketkeeper rushes in, arms in the air. Now the bowler's arrived. They're surrounding me, cheering. Eagles has his arm outstretched, finger raised, taunting me. Yeah, yeah, I get it.

Ismail *makes the long walk back to the pavilion.*

Commentator *(V/O)*   What a ripper! A disappointing start for Smiley. A duck on his debut! Looks like his footwork was all wrong there. Not something we're used to seeing with him. A young boy filled with talent. Surely nerves got the better of him there, Richie?

Ismail   My face is burning hot. I avoid everyone's eye contact, but I can feel their stares and sniggers.

Ismail *reaches the changing room. He fishes around and retrieves the borrowed box. He hurls it across the room.*

Ismail   Stupid, dirty, someone-else's, too-big box!

Ismail *rips off his pads and slumps.*

Scene Six

Later that evening. Home.

Ismail   I used to wait by the front door for my dad to get home from work, yellow plastic bat and sponge ball in hand.

Before he could even put his briefcase down, I'd have pushed him to the other end of the hallway. He'd bowl, I'd bat, and I'd race up and down in my socks and pyjamas.

Tonight, he's waiting for me.

Dad   So? How was the first match, *badshah*? Maiden century with the MRF?

Ismail   'No.'

You'd think he could read my expression. I just want to go upstairs and hide under the covers. But he won't let me.

Dad   Well? Tell me all about it! Making your debut. Must've been amazing!

Ismail   'I batted eight, couldn't find my box, and got out second ball for a duck. Happy?'

Ismail *hangs his head.*

Ismail   He puts his arm around me.

Dad   Not to worry, *beta*. You've got the whole season ahead of you. Even the best players have bad games.

Ismail   'It's not my fault! Mr Eagles hates me.'

Dad   Come on now, I'm sure that's not true, Ismail.

Ismail   'UGH you don't get it! You bought me the wrong, stupid bat and . . . you don't understand ANYTHING!'

Ismail *storms off.*

Commentator (*V/O*)   Ooo. I think he might regret that one.

//

Ismail *flops down in his room.*

Ismail   I wish I hadn't said it like that. It wasn't the bat's fault, obviously. Or my dad's.

There was nothing worse in cricket than getting out without scoring a run. A duck. It had never happened to me before. Ever. I feel like – a zero.

There's a knock at the door. **Dad** *comes in.*

Ismail   'Dad, listen. I didn't mean to say what I said. I mean, I'm so sorry for what I said . . .'

I wait for him to jump in and make an excuse for me, to take the blame on himself. But he just stands and listens.

'It's a really nice bat, Dad.'

Dad   I can send it back and get you the Newbery instead.

Ismail   He looks crushed.

'No, no, don't. I like it. I promise.'

Dad   Ismail, you know whatever happens on the cricket pitch doesn't matter.

Ismail   'It matters to me.'

Dad   What I mean is, it's more important what kind of a person you are. You're just starting to grow up. There's a long road ahead with plenty of opportunity and success, by the grace of Allah. When you look back on this, you'll laugh at how meaningless it is. May Allah have mercy on us all.

Ismail   'If Allah's so merciful, then why's he doing this to me?'

Dad   Look around you. Look at everything you've been given. Don't be ungrateful.

Ismail   'But I didn't ask for any of this! All I want is to be good at cricket.'

Dad   And you are! Blessed with talent. Have some patience. Everything will happen in good time, *insha'Allah*.

Ismail   'But this coach, Dad. He's out to get me, I swear.'

Dad   That can't be! He's there to support you. Why don't you try and explain how you're feeling. I'm sure it can be resolved. Would you like me to speak to him?

Ismail   'No! No. That won't . . .'

He thinks about explaining why, but doesn't.

Dad   You'll feel much better about all of this tomorrow.

Dad *leaves.* **Ismail** *paces, tossing a ball to himself.*

Ismail   There's no way I can sleep. I keep replaying it over and over in my head.

Commentator *(V/O)*   Here comes the next ball. Let's see what Smiley can do with it . . . And he's clean bowled him, Richie! Totally beaten for pace. Looks like his footwork was all wrong there. What a ripper! A disappointing start for Smiley. A duck on his debut.

He tries to shake off the memory. He wanders down the hallway.

Ismail   Dadi's still up.

My mum and dad brought her over from Calcutta in the late eighties. Imagine moving halfway around the world, at that age?! She hated it so much she went back after a year. But eventually, when my dada died, she was all alone, so they went and brought her back again.

He sits down next to her. They hold hands.

Ismail   'Today was rubbish, Dadi. After all that. I let everyone down. I'm sorry. I know it's my fault, I'm the batsman. But this coach is getting in my head. Every look he gives me, everything he says to me, it feels off. Wrong. I dunno. Dad thinks I should talk to him. What do you think? Maybe he'll understand? We're both batsmen. I'm sure he's had a duck in his career. Might be easier to wait and see how the next match goes. I can fix it myself. It's just one innings.'

They sit in silence.

Ismail   She gives my hand a tight squeeze and a kiss on the forehead.

Scene Seven

Monday. School.

Ismail *waits outside a classroom.* **Eagles** *appears.*

Ismail   'Sir? Could I have a moment?'

Eagles   Err . . .

Ismail   'It's Smiley, Sir.'

Eagles   Ah yes.

They walk and talk. **Ismail** *falls into step next to* **Eagles***.*

Ismail   'Sir, about the last game . . . I just think a couple of things didn't really go my way . . . I couldn't find my box and . . . I'd never batted down the order before, so I wasn't prepared to go in, and . . .'

They stop. **Ismail** *catches his breath.*

Ismail   'All to mean that I'm hoping I can prove to you why Mr Campbell chose me to join the team.'

Eagles *gives one of his trademark lingering stares.*

Eagles   I'm not looking for excuses, boy.

Ismail   'Quite, Sir. I'm not making excuses, more trying to find a way to explain . . . for us to understand one another better.'

Eagles   That's very . . . enthusiastic of you.

Ismail   I can't tell if he's being serious or sarcastic. Everything he says sounds like a joke. But not funny.

I follow him into his office. It's lined with boxes. I can see a shirt poking out with 'Cricket Tour Barbados 2005' written under the crest. I'd completely forgotten!

Eagles   Tell me, boy. Are your parents putting pressure on you?

Ismail   'No, Sir . . .'

Eagles   I know a lot of Asian parents are extremely pushy when it comes to their children's education.

Ismail   What's he talking about?

'Not at all, Sir.'

Eagles *smiles.*

Eagles   Great. In that case, let me offer you some advice.

Ismail   'Absolutely, Sir. I'm all ears.'

Eagles   Put your head down and work hard in the nets. Clean up a few things.

Ismail   Clean up a few things? He'd barely even seen me bat.

Eagles   I've seen players like you before. Bit flashy. Looking for runs on every ball. I'd like to see a little less flair and a bit more technique.

Commentator (*V/O*)   Bit harsh, don't you think, Richie?

Ismail   My face starts burning.

'Sir, if I may. I'm not sure you've had that much of a chance to see what I'm capable of. You've barely looked at me in the nets.'

Eagles   I've seen enough. And let me remind you, I know a thing or two. Do you think you're the first player with a bit of talent to come along? Talent is fleeting. Talent is essential, but it's not everything. And arrogance isn't the same as ability.

Commentator (*V/O*)   Ouch. That one's bound to sting, Mark.

Ismail   Was I being arrogant?

Eagles *is done dispensing advice.*

Eagles   Now don't be late for your next lesson, Hamza.

Ismail's *ears ring.*

Ismail   'It's . . . err . . . Ismail, Sir. Smiley.'

Eagles   Right.

Ismail *wanders out of his office in a daze.*

Ismail   Hamza?

Commentator (*V/O*)   Wonder how he's got Smiley's name mixed up there, Richie. Seems easy enough to remember.

Ismail   I bump into Finn in the hallway.

Finn   Alright, Smiley?

Ismail *barely registers.*

Finn   Had a fifty on Saturday. And a couple of wickets. Opposition were total rubbish, mind, but still . . .

Ismail   'Good for you, Finn . . .'

He keeps talking but I don't register. All I can hear are Eagles' words. 'Arrogance isn't the same as ability.'

Scene Eight

Saturday. The next match.

Ismail *sits in the pavilion, in his pads and helmet, covered in dirt. He looks dishevelled.*

Commentator (*V/O*)   I can't quite believe what I've just seen, Richie! Let's have another look at it, shall we?

Smiley Akhtar's come into bat, with another tight run chase on. He's in at the non-striker's end.

As the bowler's run in, Smiley's backing up, looking for a quick single.

Nothing wrong with that, Mark. Coming off a disappointing duck in his first match, Smiley clearly eager to get on strike and score some runs.

Indeed, Richie. Let's take a look at what happened next. It's a quick delivery, well-pitched. Laurence has played a clipped, straight drive back down the pitch towards the bowler. And this is where all hell breaks loose. The ball, travelling at some speed, has taken a dodgy bounce and veered left, crashing into what looks to be Smiley's big toe. It dribbles back towards the stumps at the bowler's end, where Smiley's now well out of his crease.

Smiley's tried his best to turn and get back, but it's all a bit hopeless really. He's thrown himself towards the line, but before he gets there, the ball's caromed into the stumps and dislodged one of the bails! The appeal goes up and Mr Eagles is quick to give the signal.

Everything that could have gone wrong has done for Smiley. Out for zero, without even facing a ball! The strangest of circumstances. Not something you see every day, even at this level, is it, Richie?

Not what we were expecting and certainly not what he had hoped for. What a shame. A terrible piece of luck for Smiley Akhtar. Another duck. Not a great start to his season so far.

Scene Nine

Later. The duck pond, St. James's Park.

Ismail *is still in his dirty cricket whites. He's down in the dumps.*

Ismail   So yeah. That happened.

I didn't even wait for the match to end. I packed up and left as quick as I could.

I can't face going home. I know what's waiting for me there. More smiles, more encouragement. The last thing I want.

I just sort of wandered around for a bit until I ended up here. The duck pond in St. James's Park. We used to have to do laps of it for PE in first year. Now it was the go-to spot for smokers.

He gives them a nod.

Ismail   I cannot believe what has just happened. It's like a freak accident mixed with a nightmare. I was trying my hardest to get on strike, to show Mr Eagles that I could bat, that I deserved a place higher up the order . . . I tried so hard I made a complete fool of myself!

He looks out at the ducks.

Ismail   I used to bat left-handed. But when I started playing more seriously, my dad decided it would be better if I switched. I'm right-handed after all. I was too young to really know, or care. I just sort of did it.

I can't stop thinking about it. I dunno why. It just keeps popping into my head.

It gets dark. **Ismail** *drags himself homeward.*

Scene Ten

Later. Home.

Ismail   I'm hoping everyone's gone to bed by the time I get back. No such luck.

Dad   There's my little master!

Ismail   'Dad, please. I really don't want to talk about cricket.'

Dad   Oh.

Ismail   'In fact, I'm quitting the team.'

Dad   What? Because of some bad batting?

Ismail   'Why not?'

Dad   When life is difficult, we must dig deep and find strength, not give up.

Ismail   'Easy for you to say. I'm the one dealing with all this. Your life is fine and dandy.'

Ismail *goes to leave.*

Dad   Hah! My son, you don't know how easy you've got it.

Ismail *is caught off guard.*

Dad   Hang on. Humour your old pop for just a minute, would you?

Ismail *reluctantly sits down.*

Dad   Ismail, do you know who Norman Tebbit is?

Ismail   'No.'

I really hope this doesn't have anything to do with Sachin Tendulkar.

Dad   Norman Tebbit was a Conservative MP. About fifteen years ago, right around the same time as you were born actually, he came up with an answer for 'dealing' with immigrants in this country. Why he decided it needed dealing with is a whole other matter . . .

Ismail *is barely paying attention.*

Ismail   After the day I've had, now a history lecture.

Dad   Here's where it gets interesting.

Ismail   At least we agree it isn't so far.

Dad   Tebbit's idea was to ask people who'd migrated here who they supported in cricket. To figure out how loyal we were. If we supported England, OK! If not, he said we'd never fit into the British way of life.

Ismail   I've never heard my dad talk like this.

Dad   I moved to London thirty-five years ago, and this man says that I'm not welcome here because of who I support in cricket?!

Ismail   'Is that why you don't support England then?'

Dad   That's not the point. I'm explaining this to show you that no matter how long we've been here, no matter what we've done or achieved, not a single day goes by without a reminder that we may never truly belong in this country.

Ismail   'So I shouldn't support England. Should I?'

Dad   It's not as simple as that! There will always be people, like Tebbit, telling us how to behave. If you want to support India, or England, that's your choice. No one can take that away from you.

Ismail *looks embarrassed.*

Ismail   'I wish you had told me about this before.'

Dad   I'm sorry. We don't always know.

Ismail   'I'm not a child anymore.'

Dad   I have to keep reminding myself that.

They sit in silence.

Dad   We've done our best to give you every chance to have a life that's better than ours. Things have changed a lot since 1970. *Insha'Allah* they continue to. Don't give up on your dreams, Ismail. Don't throw away the opportunities that God has given you. You're so lucky to have them.

Ismail   That sounds more like my dad. This time, I understand his words a bit better.

Scene Eleven

Monday. Cricket nets.

Ismail *knocks in his new bat.*

Ismail   I got my first proper bat when I was eight. A Slazenger V100. I couldn't wait to take it out, but my dad wouldn't let me play with it for a month! He taught me how treat it with linseed oil and then spend hours knocking it in.

I still feel awful, obviously. Two ducks in a row. And that's without the craziness of how I got out in the last game. But I'm trying to look ahead. What's passed is past. And it can't get any worse. Things can only go up from here.

A few of the others start to arrive. I brace myself for their ridicule after the shambles on Saturday. It doesn't take long.

Chuckers *gestures at* **Ismail**'s *bat.*

Chuckers   What's the point in that mate? Praying to Krishna to save you from another duck?

The others snigger.

Commentator *(V/O)*   Thing is, Richie, Krishna is a Hindu God while Smiley is, of course, Muslim. Chuckers' dad must've slipped the bursar something on the side to get past the entrance exams. Barely two brain cells to rub together.

Chuckers   MRF? What's that?

Ismail   'You can only get it in India. It's handmade.'

Pimmers *calls out.*

Pimmers   What, in a sweatshop?

Commentator *(V/O)*   A lazy, bigoted remark there, Mark. It's a shame to see such ignorance directed at his young teammate.

More laughter. **Ismail** *grabs it back.*

Ismail   'Oi. Shut it. Tendulkar has one.'

He goes back to knocking it in.

Ismail   I see Finn heading this way.

He waves out.

Ismail   He's got something tucked under his arm.

'What's that?'

He pulls out none other than the Newbery fucking Hammer.

Finn   Oh yeah. Dad's friends with someone over there. He sent some things to try out.

Ismail   I'm distracted by Eagles' arrival. I instantly feel a pit in my stomach.

Finn *tries to get* **Ismail**'s *attention.*

Finn   Smiley, by the way /

Ismail   'I can't talk right now, Finn.'

He brushes him off and joins the huddle.

Eagles   Great win on Saturday, boys. We really recovered well despite some, mishaps.

Ismail   Everything he says feels like a dig at me.

Eagles   . . . Let's start by offering a big welcome to the newest member of the team, Finley!

Ismail   What?

He turns around.

Ismail   Finn is smiling. The others cheer and clap. Eagles gestures Finn over and puts his arm around him. Is this a joke?

They break into nets. **Ismail** *wanders off to the side. He sits down and resumes knocking his bat in, staring at* **Finn**. **Finn** *comes over. He's ecstatic.*

Finn   Great news, isn't it?

Commentator (*V/O*)   I think Smiley's trying his hardest to fake a smile there, but . . . ooo, it's just not happening for him. No one's going to believe that, are they, Richie?

Ismail   'Why didn't you tell me?'

Finn   It just happened this morning.

Ismail *does not match his enthusiasm.*

Ismail   'Yeah . . . so about the Ashes. I can't go with you anymore.'

Finn   Oh! How come?

Ismail   'Just can't. England's going to get smashed anyway.'

Finn   Smiley, is everything alright?

Ismail   Yeah, I'm fine. I just don't support England, so I don't care about the Ashes. In case you hadn't noticed, I'm Indian.

He waves the MRF at him.

Finn   OK . . .

Ismail *gets up.*

Ismail   Over at the nets, Chuckers calls out to me.

Chuckers   Come on, Smelly!

Ismail   What did he say? He and Pimmers are laughing their heads off.

Ismail *strides over to them.*

Ismail   'What did you call me?'

Chuckers   Nothing, nothing . . .

Ismail   'Yes you did.'

Chuckers   It's just a joke, Smelly. I mean Smiley.

He snorts with laughter.

Ismail   I shove him in the chest, hard.

'Don't call me that.'

Chuckers   Watch it, Smelly Shit.

Ismail   I shove him again.

'I said don't call me that.'

Chuckers *turns to the rest of the team.*

Chuckers   What do we think, people? Cos he looks like shit, and he plays like shit. Seems like he's a smelly shit to me.

Ismail   Everyone falls about laughing. I look at Finn. He doesn't say a word. I stare at him. But he's looking anywhere else than back at me.

Eagles is standing right there, saying nothing.

Ismail *approaches* **Eagles**.

Ismail   'Sir, Chuckers just called me a Smelly Shit.'

Eagles   What are you talking about?

Ismail   'The others . . . Sir . . . they're saying . . . things. About me. I need you to ask them to stop.'

Eagles   Come on, boy! I'm sure it's just some playful banter. Give it back to them.

Ismail   'But Sir!'

Eagles   Listen, if you're finding it too difficult, I can always send you back down to the Under Fifteens . . .

Ismail *turns back to the others.*

Ismail   'Hey! Listen here!'

He gets their attention.

Ismail   'You've got the wrong guy. Get this.'

He glances at **Finn**.

Ismail   'Did you know, Finn here, slept over at my house once. And the next day, my mum found his underwear hidden in the corner of my bedroom. COVERED IN SHIT!'

The others are stunned into silence.

Ismail   Everyone's mouths are hanging wide open.

'. . . And I'm not talking a skid mark. I mean like a full-on turd. A proper sausage.'

Ismail *waits, desperate for their reaction. Eventually, they burst into laughter.*

Chuckers   Finn, the follow-through farter!

The rest of the team are in stitches. **Ismail** *wanders away, relieved.*

Ismail   It happened years ago. I kept it to myself all this time. I'd not even mentioned it to Finn. And he never once thanked me.

The First XI was my thing. How dare he come in here and try to steal it? I look over in his direction. His face is bright red. That'll tell him.

Chuckers bounds over. He slaps me across the back.

Chuckers   Good one, Smiley!

Ismail *gives him a nod.*

Commentator (*V/O*)   Well, Richie, Smiley's going to have to live with the consequences of that one. Not his finest moment, throwing his best friend to the lions to save his own skin.

Ismail (*to* **Commentator**)   I had to! What choice did I have? I'm not losing my place in the team.

A solitary quack. **Ismail** *shoots a glare in its direction.*

Ismail   Easy for you to say.

Scene Twelve

A couple of weeks later. The next match. It's drizzling.

Ismail *is fielding. He stands around, bored. He sucks loudly on a Cherry Drop.*

Ismail   There's nothing worse than fielding in the rain. Especially if you've been standing around the whole game like me. I guess this is what other people usually feel like.

Finn and I haven't spoken in two weeks, which feels like a year. I regret telling everyone about what had happened. But at least it got people off my back.

He pops in another Cherry Drop.

Ismail   Out of nowhere, the batsman sweeps the ball towards me. Finally!

Commentator (*V/O*)   It looks like he hasn't caught hold of this one. It's a thick edge and the ball's gone sky high. Smiley Akhtar's underneath it.

Ismail *looks to the sky, trying to judge where the ball's going to land.*

Commentator (*V/O*)   He might've misjudged it, Richie. He's having to race in . . . Oh, now he's dived for it, full stretch.

He races in, and dives at full stretch.

Commentator (*V/O*)   He's caught it! Has he? What a catch!

Ismail *lies in the dirt, clutching the ball in his hands.*

Ismail   'HOWZAAAT!!!'

It's a spectacular catch! I wait for my teammates to mob me.

Silence.

Commentator (*V/O*)   Wait, no! Mr Eagles has signalled not out! Well, Richie, we'll have to have another look at that. I was sure he'd got his hands underneath it.

Ismail *gets up and rushes over to* **Eagles**.

Ismail   'What do you mean, not out?'

Eagles   The ball hit the ground first.

Commentator (*V/O*)   Things are getting a bit testy, Mark.
There's no action replay to look at, but I can confirm that it
was indeed a catch.

Ismail *thrusts the ball in front of* **Eagles'** *face.*

Ismail   'No it didn't. I caught it. Look!'

Eagles *smirks and moves* **Ismail'***s hand away.*

Eagles   I've told you, it's not out. Now get on with the
game, boy.

Ismail   'I caught it. I appealed for it, because I caught it. I
wouldn't appeal for a wicket if it wasn't out. I have more
class than that.'

Eagles   You're not acting very classy right now, are you?
The umpire's decision is final. Stop being so petulant, boy.

Ismail   'Either I caught it fair and square, or I didn't, and
I'm cheating.'

Ismail *gets no response.*

Ismail   'So you're calling me a cheat?'

'You're calling me a cheat.'

'YOU'RE CALLING ME A CHEAT?'

Ismail *storms off.*

Commentator (*V/O*)   Well, Richie, I can't remember a
moment like this in all my years. Oh! Smiley's just gone and
kicked the stumps! The bails have almost hit Eagles in the
face there! Wow! That's quite the reaction. And now, he's
walking off the pitch! He's walked right off the pitch in what
seems to be a protest of the decision! Incredible scenes here!

I can't quite believe my eyes, Mark. Smiley's walked out of
the gates, onto the pavement, and across the road. He's not
stopping. He's still holding onto the match ball.

Ismail   My eyes are flooded with tears. I barely even know what's happening. I run. I can't see where I'm going. I run and run and cry and run.

He runs until he's out of breath. He doubles over, panting. When he catches his breath, he looks around to see where he is.

Ismail   My feet bring me right back to the duck pond.

He looks at the cricket ball he's gripping in his hand.

Ismail (*muttering*)   'Catches win matches.'

He heaves it as far as he can into the pond. The ducks scatter, quacking loudly. He wipes away his tears and flops down.

Scene Thirteen

7 July 2005. The duck pond, St. James's Park. Morning.

We've returned to the opening scene. **Ismail** *is in school uniform. He feeds the ducks.*

Ismail   So now you know. It's been quite the summer. Do you reckon I can get into *Wisden* for throwing the biggest fit ever seen on a cricket pitch?

The morning after, I got to the entrance to school, and then . . . kept walking straight past it. Came here instead.

It keeps happening. Most days. I get up, fully intending to go in. Then I arrive and something comes over me. I just can't deal with it right now. It's better here. It's calm. Gives me time to think.

How long had people been calling me Smelly Shit? My teammates . . . I still can't believe I told them about Finn. The whole memory is blurred. All I remember is knowing I had to do something to make it stop.

What if I never played cricket again? I think I'd be fine with it. After everything that's happened, the last place in the universe I want to be is back at nets, or anywhere in sight of a cricket pitch. Not that they'd have me anyway.

I've been trying to figure out why I freaked out like that. Being accused of cheating, it did something to me. I'd never cheat. I didn't need to. And for everyone to think I had . . . it hurts.

He replays the catch.

Ismail   It was an amazing catch though. The sort of moment that can really lift your spirits, you know? Just what I had needed. And Eagles, that petty, evil man, had ripped it away from me. I just know if anyone else had caught it . . .

He doesn't finish his thought. Big Ben bongs in the background.

Ismail   Latin first lesson. Sir never takes the register. I bet no one's even noticed I'm not there.

All of a sudden, sirens blare from every direction. **Ismail** *gets to his feet, looking around. It's a huge commotion.*

Ismail   What's going on?!

Policemen appear.

Policeman   DON'T MOVE!!!

Ismail *freezes.*

Commentator *(V/O)*   It looks like . . . a big commotion unfolding here, Richie! Smiley Akhtar's being arrested?! Oh . . . news reports coming in . . .

Blackout.

//

RECORDING: *The following are excerpts from recordings of conversations between the playwright and members of the creative team about their experiences in and around the events of 7/7.*

Sharjil   Whenever these things happen, even if you're not involved with them, when you hear stuff on the news, your first thought is wow, that's just happened, and, you know, you kind of think of what it must be like, and then, my secondary thought is always, I hope it's not a Muslim . . . I hope it's not a Muslim. That's the thing you always worry about the most. I suppose, with your affiliation to your own religion, you don't want your religion to be involved in it.

Maariyah   Instantly, you would see him and recognise that he was a Muslim man. But he's also a paramedic going and saving lives after these horrific terrorist attacks done in theory in the name of Islam. It must've been a very strange experience for him, being like, I'm here to protect and save and help people, but I know as soon as I'm out of this uniform, that I'm going to be seen as a threat.

Sharjil   I'm a paramedic with twenty-six years of experience, working solely in London for the ambulance service, and I attended the 7/7 bombings . . .

Maryam   But, you know, you're kind of aware of how your Muslimness affects you after an event like that . . .

Ibraheem   Yeah, it was just . . . it was just crazy how that single moment, like, changed . . .

Maryam   . . . Especially like, the men in my family, were treated, you know, by police . . . or especially in airports and things like that . . . there were lots of incidents where then it was explained to us, like, you know, it's because we're Muslims and that's why we're being targeted in that way.

Holly   Just a constant, uncomfortable, like, 'where are you from?' 'Where are you from?' But my brother, it was like, you're a potential threat. You're a Brown man, with a beard and it's threatening.'

Ibraheem   . . . Like, I noticed so many people staring at us, like I even noticed an old man, like – I distinctly remember, 'why don't these people just go back to where they came from?' I remember that.

Maariyah   . . . And he's walking towards the bus, and then, a bunch of armed police officers stopped him. And was like, 'why are they stopping me?' And when he was telling me the story, I was like, oh my God, like, is it because he's Muslim and they think . . .

Sharjil   You're quite aware of how people perceive you.

Hamza   Well I think, as I've grown up, I've become more attuned to my identity as a British Muslim. And the closer I've got to that, the more significant 7/7 has become as an event.

//

Scene Fourteen

A few hours later. Police station.

Ismail *sits alone in a holding cell.*

Ismail   I've always been known for my timing. It's what makes me a great batsman. When you time it well, it's like everything becomes slow motion and you've got a million years to see the ball all the way onto the middle of the bat, then effortlessly racing to the boundary.

Today, I've got the worst timing known to man. At least that's what the policemen who arrested me keep saying. Once they believed me. I told them the truth. That I was meant to be at school. I don't know why they won't just let me leave.

I've never been in a police station before. I can hear my dad's voice in my head. Just say *insha'Allah*, and everything will be fine. I've been repeating it over and over in my head since they put me in handcuffs. *Insha'Allah. Insha'Allah. Insha'Allah.*

Finally, the door opens. He looks up.

Ismail   What? It's Mr fucking Eagles!

'What are you doing here?'

Eagles   I can go if you don't need me.

Ismail   'No! I mean why did they call you?'

Eagles *waves a piece of paper at him.*

Eagles   They found this in your stuff.

Ismail   He's holding a team sheet from our last match with his name and phone number at the bottom. Just my luck.

'So can we go?'

Eagles   They said it'll take a few minutes.

Ismail   'What for?'

Eagles *shrugs and smirks.*

Ismail   That smirk. It gets me every time. I can feel myself losing control.

'What's your problem?'

That gets his attention.

Eagles   Excuse me?

Ismail   'Why do you hate me? Since the first time we met, you've had it in for me. What is your problem? Just tell me!'

Eagles *is as calm as can be.*

Eagles   I've got nothing against you, boy. Maybe if you stopped feeling so sorry for yourself all the time, you'd actually get somewhere.

Ismail   There it is. That word. Boy.

'My name is ISMAIL. Not "boy." Definitely not Hamza. It's ISMAIL.'

Silence.

Ismail   'And I know why you hate me. It's because I'm Indian.'

No response.

Ismail   'You don't like me because I'm Indian. I know it. I just know it. That's why you said I didn't take that catch.'

Ismail *hangs his head.*

Eagles   Have you finished?

Silence.

Eagles   What an absurd thing to say. It's never even crossed my mind. I treat everyone the same. Makes no difference. It's your entitlement, that's your issue. In my day, everybody knew their place. You don't just get to play on my team. You have to earn it, like everyone else. I didn't become the best batsman in school history by whining. I did it with hard work and performance.

Ismail   'Yeah, well, you didn't have to deal with a racist coach.'

Eagles   What a pathetic excuse. So ungrateful. You're lucky to even be at this school. And then you come along and make accusations like that. It's this sort of rubbish that damages our country and everything we stand for. Same as that lot out there blowing us up. I bet you don't even support England, do you?

Silence. **Ismail** *looks up at him.*

Ismail   'I'd like to go home now. Please.'

They head for the door. **Eagles** *opens it, then stops and looks back at* **Ismail**.

Eagles   Look at what good this has done you. I hope you've learned your lesson.

Scene Fifteen

September 2005. The duck pond, St. James's Park.

The aftermath of the Ashes' victory parade is all around. **Ismail**
wanders among the mess.

Ismail   They only went and won it. The Ashes! The first
time since 1987. The whole country went crazy. The parade
came right past school. It was total mayhem. Eventually the
teachers just let us come join in.

It was cool. Everyone came down here, and it was like a
massive party. Someone was going around painting people's
faces with England flags. Finn got one. He and I made up
over the summer, once he got back from Barbados. He even
asked me to come to the final test match with him again. In
the end, I decided not to. Ever since learning about Norman
Tebbit and the cricket test, I just felt weird about it all. And I
knew his dad would ask me who I was supporting, again.

//

Truth be told, I didn't even know if I was coming back to
school at that point. I spent a lot of time thinking about it
over the holidays. I thought I'd be in heaps of trouble after
the arrest, and everything had come out about me skipping
school. But my parents were mostly relieved I was alive.

They had a lot of questions though. I bring my dad down to
the duck pond to try and explain things for the millionth
time.

Ismail *tosses bread into the pond.*

Dad   You could've been killed, Ismail.

Ismail *rolls his eyes.*

Ismail   He's said that a lot.

Dad   And I still don't understand why you stopped going to
school.

Ismail *turns around.*

Ismail   'You put me in this school. And then you just
expected everything to be fine. Nobody understood what I

was going through. I felt so alone. I had to get away from it all.'

Dad   We only wanted the best for you.

Ismail *turns to the pond.*

Ismail   At least we were having these conversations now. Like about changing schools. My mum and dad left it up to me to decide. I was a bit worried about going back. But the summer was a long time, and I missed my friends. And by break on the first day, I fell into an old groove.

Knowing how much my parents care about my education, they must be relieved.

//

The boundary of a cricket pitch, somewhere in space and time.

Ismail *carries the MRF.*

Ismail   I still love cricket. Somehow. Despite it all.

We found out about a cricket club near our house. The team's almost entirely South Asians. We go down there to watch them play. Stand on the boundary rope. I can't remember the last time we did something like this together.

Dad   The next Sachin could be here!

He winks at **Ismail**.

Ismail   After the match, we wander around the pitch. It feels good to be out there. Familiar. But without any pressure.

'Dad, when you made me stop batting left-handed. I never really thought about it. But it would have been an advantage. I could have been an even better player.'

Dad   Yes, well . . .

Ismail   'But you didn't want me to be different, did you? I never knew it was wrong to be different.'

Dad   Don't ever think that, Ismail.

Ismail   'But it's true.'

Silence. **Ismail** *looks at his father.*

Ismail   'I just wanted to be like you.'

Ismail *sets up to bat, left-handed this time.*

Commentator (*V/O*)   Well, folks, this is certainly something unexpected. It looks like Ismail Akhtar . . . he's lined up to bat left-handed here. Just like he used to as a child. I wonder what he's trying to do. The ball's coming in now, it's short, and Ismail's quick onto it with his trademark timing. He's given this one everything he's got, looking to clear the leg-side boundary. Has he managed it?!

Ismail   Well folks, this is certainly something unexpected. I've lined up to bat left-handed here. Just like I used to as a child. The ball's coming in now. It's short, and I'm quick onto it with my trademark timing. I'm giving this one everything I've got. Looking to clear the leg side boundary. Have I managed it?

Ismail *gets on the front foot, playing a big drive. The ducks quack furiously.*

Blackout.

The End.

For a complete listing of
Methuen Drama titles, visit:
www.bloomsbury.com/drama

Follow us on Twitter and keep up to date
with our news and publications
@MethuenDrama